PORTLAND
ALIVE AT THE CENTER

PORTLAND
ALIVE AT THE CENTER

COMTEMPORARY POEMS FROM PORTLAND, OREGON

PORTLAND

EDITED BY

Susan Denning
Jesse Lichtenstein
Leah Stenson

OOLIGAN
PRESS

Portland: Alive at the Center
Contemporary Poems from Portland, Oregon
© 2013 Ooligan Press

ISBN13: 978-1-932010-57-2

Ooligan Press
Department of English
Portland State University
P.O. Box 751, Portland, Oregon 97207
503.725.9410 (phone); 503.725.3561 (fax)
ooligan@ooliganpress.pdx.edu
www.ooliganpress.pdx.edu

Library of Congress Cataloging-in-Publication Data is available by request.

Cover design by J. Adam Collins
Interior design by Poppy Milliken & Lorna Nakell

Contents

PUBLISHER'S NOTE

Welcome to the Pacific Northwest's poetry community. You hold in your hands the inaugural publication of the Pacific Poetry Project, designed to capture this moment in poetry—the early years of the twenty-first century—from a region of North America unlike any other. We hope to bring you to the poetry salons, slams, and open-mic nights that are everywhere you look.

In the fall of 2009, a dedicated bunch of poetry lovers at Ooligan Press just happened to find themselves in the midst of a discussion about the state of poetry in our hometown—Portland, Oregon—and around the Pacific Northwest. What they came to discover was that poetry was happening all over the place in a grassroots way. Poetry represents a tiny slice of the revenue generated by the publishing industry. But as a visible and active community in our home, it is flourishing and bustling, full of life and energy. In Portland, Seattle, or Vancouver, you will find a poetry event happening weekly, if not nightly. These may be in our big bookstores, or they may be at a small wine bar, or they might even be in someone's living room, but it is a constant exchange among people who love the rhythm and meter of poetic work.

Based on this realization, Ooligan Press decided to develop an anthology of contemporary poetry from the Pacific Northwest. Very quickly, however, we realized that we were trying to do too much with one book. How could we possibly capture this buzzing, vibrant community between the covers of a single book? We couldn't. But we could launch a continuing project dedicated to two things: collecting and promoting the best poetic works from our region, and making those works available to a wider realm of readers.

Our first goal is relatively simple: we want to share the best of the best with our readers. Our second goal is a little more difficult, and slightly subversive (after all, we do live in Portland). In the last twenty or thirty years, poetry has become the provenance of a few smaller, dedicated non-profit publishers, like Copper Canyon, and of big university publishers, like the University of Pittsburgh Press (which both do amazing work). But even more, poetry seems to have become an outlier; something we used to appreciate and enjoy, but can't quite connect with now. Maybe this comes from having had to read the standard poetry fare in high school or college, which had little apparent connection to our teenage selves. Or maybe this comes from the lack of exposure and mainstream popularity of poetry, which is in part due to the fact that trade publishers don't see poetry as a financially viable product.

Whatever the cause, we think it's a shame. We think it is damaging to our cultural diversity and literary culture to be exposed to less poetry and fewer poets. Because, as Robert Duncan Gray writes in the Introduction to the book in your hands, "poetry is everywhere." So why not make poetry more "accessible"? Why not treat it like a rock star, as we do with other forms of writing? That is our goal with the Pacific Poetry Project. We want to bring poetry back to the mainstream conversation. We want to re-create the dynamic and vibrant poetry nights that happen among friends, but in the pages of these books (or on the screen of your favorite reading device). We want poetry to be for the people, as it always has been. We reject the notion that you have to "get" poetry to love it. We all get poetry. We just need to be given the permission to take whatever we do away from the reading or hearing of it. So for the publications with the Pacific Poetry Project logo on them, you are hereby given permission to think your own thoughts about the work inside. There's no right answer and there's no wrong answer. We want you to come to your own conclusions. But don't stop there. Take your thoughts and share them with a friend. Make poetry part of your conversation. Quote it on your favorite social network. Give it to your friends and family.

We are on a mission to bring poetry to the people. We need your help to do it. Enjoy *Alive at the Center* and welcome to the Pacific Poetry Project.

—*Ooligan Press*

ALIVE AT THE CENTER

(AN INTRODUCTION)

Everything is super. Super duper.

Imagine Poetry (with a capital P) as a functional member of society. Poetry gets a day job and earns a sizable paycheck. Poetry purchases two luxury Mercedes Benzes and gives one to me—a brand new, shiny Mercedes Benz! Super duper. The inside smells like lavender honey. I bake Poetry a chocolate cake, by which I mean to say, Thank You. It doesn't turn out perfect, but Poetry doesn't seem to care—so nonchalant!—Poetry eats three big slices of my imperfect chocolate cake. Oh, all that chocolate all over Poetry's face!

Fantastic.

Lately I have been thinking about poetry with a lowercase p, so naturally I am worried. I have also been thinking about death, salt, and hot water—or more specifically, deathsalt and hotwater. I have written a mathematical equation:

$$p = 4(hw) + (ds)$$
Where p = poetry, h = hot, w = water, d = death and s = salt.

I have also written an accompanying recipe:

Poetry à la mode
> Combine four parts hotwater with one part deathsalt in a clean glass bowl.
> Stir vigorously with soft hands.
> Serve with ice cream.

A beekeeper friend of mine has a swarm up for grabs. I am worried about the poetry of it. I guess I am worried about the poetry fading or weakening in certain spots. What would we do for a poem compared to what we would do for, say, a taco? And is there really all that much difference between a poem and a taco?

If all the poets of the world die, what then of poetry? What if all the good poets died? Would good poetry be dead? Is poetry dependent on poets? I don't think so, but really I don't know.

I believe that poetry is not necessarily site-specific. You can find a poem anywhere. You can find ten poems in bed, an entire volume inside your kitchen—you certainly don't need to leave the house to write. There is plenty of poetry all around. Poetry tucked in the sock drawer and under the couch. Poetry amongst the sharp knives. In the bathtub—hotwater. Deathsalt in the potatoes. Nothing is safe. That being said, go outside. It's nice outside.

I find a lot of poems at work, which is a bummer because I am at work. I find poems whilst riding my bicycle, which is also a bummer because I am riding my bicycle. It is often inconvenient to write a poem. Some poems must be ignored, or rather left alone—"ignored" seems harsh. Some poems remain free and that's super. Some poems are lost and some are eternally found. Whatever. Super duper. No big deal.

Sometimes I find poems perfect and easy. Poetry can be so easy. That's a big secret. Poets don't generally like to talk about it; perhaps we worry that such a declaration might lessen the value of our work. Truth be told, sometimes poetry is piss-easy and most of the time it carries no inherent value whatsoever. I come home from work and take all my clothes off in the kitchen. I say hello to the cat. I walk through the house to the bedroom and lie down. I get high and lost in the blades of the ceiling fan. I go to the bathroom and stare at myself in the mirror for a short while. Then I return to the bedroom, lie on the bed and the rest of the evening is all about poetry. I walk naked from room to room and find poems waiting for me. Eager poems rolling around. Belly-up poems. I hardly write, yet at the end of the night I have accumulated twenty poems or more! It must be some kind of magic.

Poetry is everywhere.

I once watched Ed Skoog recite poems in the middle of the night in an underground parking lot. I once watched Emily Kendal Frey recite poems on the third floor of a shopping mall. It happens in the weirdest places, under the most unlikely circumstances. Poetry seems to be all around, occupying the spaces in which we least expect to find it.

So here we are.

You hold in your hands a flock of poems. A gathering, yes. An organized pastiche poured fresh from the top left corner of America. American poetry is alive and well. American poetry is healthy. There is so damn much of it! How does this happen? A great many people share this huge experience, some sort of life in America, and feel the urge to report back. There are things here we feel must be shared, passed on. It is a beautiful thing. Super.

Upon reading this collection, one cannot help but feel a great sense of relief. Everything is super. Poetry is fat and fun and full of beauty. Super duper. The problems we face today are bigger and more complicated than those we faced yesterday, but rest assured—there is poetry in between, around and inside everything, and every day we are getting better and better at exposing it. Everything is going to be just fine.

I have written a recipe for this book.

Alive at the Center

Combine four parts hotwater, one part deathsalt, a dash of fresh ginger, a clove of crushed garlic, five pickled pigs feet, one sea anemone, three tusks, two bundles of cashmere, a pint of Puget Sound, a rumble of kitten purr, a chorus of traffic jam, two pocketfuls of lavender honey, a whalebone of satisfied hunger and two feet of sadness, a lungfull of unmelodious childsong, a mile of rusted train track, a never ending ambulance siren, two slices of cold cheese pizza, raw beef on the edge, fresh hoof, warm blood of beet, nine bridges, a dash of Douglas Fir, a waterfall of black coffee and one day-old donut. Salt and pepper to taste. Stir vigorously with soft hands. Serve with ice cream and imperfect chocolate cake.

Everything is super.

—*Robert Duncan Gray*

Portland

POEMS FROM PORTLAND, OREGON

We put together a selection of Portland poets. Some of them don't live here, but they belong to us. Some of them live close by—Eugene, Corvallis, Monmouth—we share the Willamette Valley. They're ours.

Sometimes they refer to poets of any given region as a tribe. It kind of bugs me. I'm not sure why. When people refer to the tribe of poets, I think of Liam Neeson in *Rob Roy*, with men in kilts roaming the Scottish Highlands. I fear we lack the wardrobe to really be called tribal.

The Cosmic Baseball Association is an online fantasy baseball team, made up of poets, philosophers, and artists. Imagining the poets of Portland as a baseball team seems a little more appropriate. For example:

> Walt Curtis thinks playing baseball is a super fantastic terrific idea and is flirting with the umpire, but really just wants to make sure no one gets hurt. Mary Szybist is pitching fastballs, and Paulann's bat just made contact. Biespiel's running towards the fence.
>
> Jesse reminds us how incredibly cool we all are, even when we feel like total doofuses in the outfield. Carl and Crystal were radiant and rapt while we explained the rules to them, but they've been running around the backstop and tripping the catcher all afternoon.

Of course the metaphor gets forced at a certain point. The poets of this region are no more a baseball team than we are an ancient tribe. No, wait—we are. We're a tribe, a baseball team, we're an organized, inept crime syndicate, we're transparently ambitious used car salesmen, we're an off-key, melodic high school choir. We're an extended family with relatives that inspire, confuse, frustrate us—but we always invite them home for Thanksgiving because it wouldn't be a celebration without them.

We're in collusion and opposition. We meant to come to your reading but couldn't get the baby to sleep, had to prepare for class tomorrow, had to mow the lawn—but could you please just take a moment to read this poem we wrote yesterday? We think it's really good—does the ending seem forced? We came to your reading and your work was so amazing we decided there was no point in trying to write another poem ever again. You were just that brilliant and we secretly started wishing you'd leave town—no, not really. We were proud to live in the same town with you—to know we might see you writing at a table in our neighborhood coffee shop, we might run into you at Powell's—and we went home and stayed up all night. We stole all your metaphors and witty asides, and made them ours. We knew you wouldn't mind.

I don't know if Portland poets write with their landscape in mind. Some of them can't escape it, and some of them are confounded by other things.

So sure, it's Oregon, go ahead—mention the rain and the Doug Firs and the fish and the rivers that run through it all. Some of us can't help but notice these things. Thank you for noticing them in a way that reminds us why we can't take them for granted, that reminds us why Tom McCall called this Eden.

But also remember—this is Stumptown. A long time ago people came here and cut down all the trees, so they could build some houses, stick around awhile.

So if you don't know if a steelhead is a salmon or a trout, and you keep forgetting what deciduous means, consider the names of some of our reading series: Loggernaut, If Not For Kidnap, Spare Room, Mountain Writers, Bad Blood. Consider the names of some of the poems found here: *Dismantling. Enlightment. Accidents of Trees. Distant Friends. Exile Off Foster.*

The poets of Portland are waiting for you.

—*Susan Denning*

A MAN WHO WAS AFRAID OF LANGUAGE

The houses, the trees, and the dust had become
Sentences having nothing to do with themselves.
He seldom left his apartment now, the only refuge

He could endure, the dank spaces
And dim lights, the phone and radio unplugged.
Even printed works went on shifting

And crossing while stray phrases, echoes of phrases
Took up the burden. He tried to think
Of the same thing again and again.

He closed the blinds, but the boys still came
With their taunts and jokes and vulgar songs.
Sunlight slanted into their eyes.

A woman in blue made ambiguous gestures.

ACCIDENTS OF TREES

In columns and rows
they grew sideways for spite
or confusion, elbowed
for light.

In these tidy rows the whippoorwills
disorient and cannot rest.

The dust boiled as they fell
into square bright pools of field.

The wild trees, not far away,
stood on tiptoe. The new ones
in delicate tangles of root
where the nurses once fed them,
and old survivors licked black
where they'd opened their skirts.

Toward the straight forest
long throats leaned forward
shushing the birds.

Daneen Bergland

ANNUNCIATION: EVE TO AVE

The wings behind the man I never saw.
But often, afterward, I dreamed his lips,
Remembered the slight angle of his hips,
His feet among the tulips and the straw.

I liked the way his voice deepened as he called.
As for the words, I liked the showmanship
With which he spoke them. Behind him, distant ships
Went still; the water was smooth as his jaw—

And when I learned that he was not a man—
Bullwhip, horsewhip, unzip, I could have crawled
Through thorn and bee, the thick of hive, rosehip,
Courtship, lordship, gossip and lavender.
(But I was quiet, quiet
As eagerness—that astonished, dutiful fall.)

APPETITE

Pale gold and crumbling with crust
mottled dark, almost bronze,
pieces of honeycomb lie on a plate.
Flecked with the pale paper
of hive, their hexagonal cells
leak into the deepening pool
of amber. On your lips,
against palate, tooth and tongue,
the viscous sugar squeezes
from its chambers, sears sweetness
into your throat until you chew
pulp and wax from a blue city
of bees. Between your teeth
is the blown flower and the flower's
seed. Passport pages stamped
and turning. Death's officious hum.
Both the candle and its anther
of flame. Your own yellow hunger.
Never say you can't take
this world into your mouth.

Paulann Petersen

AVULSION

And though I grieved, my time in hell
was sure and short. Those gaseous veins
of gorgeous mineral states told me more
than I could know on the sedgy plains of earth.

There was no voice like yours
in hell. The saxophones were verdigris
and cold. There was no voice at all,
not yours, and not my own.

I cannot say whose empty house it was
that burned throughout the wrinkled night.
I can tell you that morning brought intelligent
blue light not seen by anyone on earth.

I don't remember much—just this:
the lid was screwed on tight
and no one cared if heaven fell
to earth or gathered us in light.

BETWEEN BRANCHES AND WIND

Escucha, sólo escucha el estruendo del oleaje, mientras el
mirlo clama entre las ramas y el viento.
—Jaime Luís Huenún

leapt, this time, into a space that had been
 assembling, as had we, gathering
in particles and
    in the dark, a space
against

which we might come
            and, bracketed
 by raw limbs
above us,
allied in a null state, here
 in movement and in a temp-

orary rise
 beyond will,
expedience, charge,
   let enter us what was carried on
the air: the least
syllable, its least counterpart.

after-
image of a wing that in lifting
 also masks
its voice. this view is a
void,
a sway or
its echo, and all of it a
   relative still-
ness carved, we say,
for us, the long

Jesse Lichtenstein

tail
of a crash, a line of
decay, if unbroken,
bursting at the end into
  glitter,
running in, as a condition,
as motor and
  as fuel for
wind,
the stunter of the branch under
which we keep
a safe
distance—
and from each

other:
sound of a making
and slower
unmaking, breaking, within
  and beneath, as we
know, the same
wheel.

BLOODLINE

The moon is wet nurse
to roses. She suckles
each soft-mouthed poppy.

Blame her for menses.
Rail at her for the craving
to binge and purge.

Please her when you choose
to delay the day for planting,
biding your time
until night has fattened
her silver torso. Praise her
when the fleck of seed
poked down into damp dark
takes hold and swells.

Any girl-child is always
her offspring.

Upbraid her for your daughter's
sass and door-slams,
that hot hurry to be what most
differs from you.

Long ago, the moon decided
on a pathway against the route
stars take. No one else
would dare to walk
the black sky backward.

Paulann Petersen

BLOOM AND DECAY

1

These twisted ivy patches are not a tale of pursuit, and any unraveling
That binds us—rituals of envy, outlived slurs, old burns—
Has us stomaching odd moods that we get sick over but still obey.
If you silence the sky, my love, I'll close the boulevard down.
If you run hard in sleet and wind, then walk out of your life,
I'll stop at last in this city and die.

2

All evening now this city has been closer at hand and shinier—
The understory leaving us inseparable and maddened—
While the flinty candlelights in the window thin and canter,
Bloom and decay, and without question
Our eyes have opened to blackness and what is left unsaid:
This passage of delight is our sorrow and our bed.

BORING

I was going to say something, but it was boring.
It's more interesting if you wonder what it was.
Birds are boring, unless they're indoors.
Paper is a little less boring when it's folded into animals.
I bought a plant and its pot was terra cotta,
which is boring, so I painted it. This made the plant
look boring, so I painted it too—you know the rest.
My old car was rusted in spots, so I added a stripe.
Is it excited that racing days lie ahead? Probably not.
My boss is boring, so when he talks
I imagine a polar bear behind him.
Steve Martin wished for a month-long orgasm,
but that would get boring after a week or so.
You should think of what you find boring.
This thing right here is boring, you were just thinking,
which is wonderful—it's all part of the experience.
Sandwiches bore me to sleep. Sleep is never boring.
Computers are deathly boring, so I keep thinking
of painting over mine's plastic beige with a woodland scene
in spastic kid colors, but I haven't found the time.
I love everything very poorly.

COUNTRY MUSIC

When the dark finds us
full-throated, singing
of bright mother & river-dead men,
& our dim Audrey lost to another,
let the words bless us
somehow, a ceiling of fire
above our heads—
& let The Caller huddle near
with his ether strings, his beautiful
wounds, his waves of grass
Let us hang in the night until this passes.

DISMANTLING

Call Joel (eves) 623-9765

Smack in the public eye
at Ninth and Van Buren, tearing down
an old house—
"Not demolition, dismantling!" says Joel. Slowly
we make the house disappear.
It takes a few months.
We do this for a living.
                          Our sign says:
USED LUMBER FOR SALE.
Neat stacks of it on the front lawn
around a dormant forsythia—
shiplap and siding, and over here
we have two-by...
That pile is already sold.

We also have toilets, sinks, remarkable
savings on bent nails,
French doors, free kindling
and more. Lots more.

            ...

With the roof off
a house looks more like a cathedral,
rafters outlined against the sky.
A pair of ragged priests,
we celebrate
nothing stick by stick. We are making the shape of
nothing,
creating
an absence.

Clemens Starck

And when we have finished,
what will there be at Ninth and Van Buren?
A square of bare earth
where a house was.
Sidewalk. Foundation. Concrete stoop.
Two steps up
and you're there.

DISTANT FRIENDS

That year we both lost fathers, even though,
natural aristocrat, you didn't say so
and I spoke of nothing else. For me

the world was like a country road running
between field burns gone out of control, turning
the air acrid and opaque with smoke,

and what I mourned—lost comfort or stove-in
safety, haven, or, more simply, the loving—
I could not say then. Now, years later,

I wonder at you, seeming so able
outwardly, but underneath like a small bull
terrier wrestling with an intruder

or bone. It still seems a kind of wisdom
to me looking back: such delicate tact or calm,
practiced loss dexterously plowed under.

Lisa Steinman

DON'T ASK, DON'T TELL

It's all gray at the bridge toll backup. It's winter,
it's always winter here, and raining hard,
when it's your turn to drive.

Your new rideshare companion curls up like a cat
in the heated leather seat beside you. Asian,
though French you guess from her purr.

She's twenty, maybe twenty-four. You found her
on Craigslist. You know nothing about her
and of course she knows nothing of you.

She's comfortable enough in your escort—she's
slowly nodding off—but when you reach down
for the stick, she grips the leather strap of her

black workbag a little harder, as if rendered
by an early morning dream that has returned
and taken hold.

You turn up the heat and she breathes uneasily,
shifts in her seat. Though when her flushed
cheek turns, she smiles like daybreak, breath

tinctured with sage, raspberry, warm Belgian
chocolate—It doesn't matter that you could be her
father, or her mother. It doesn't matter if you are a

woman, or a man. The distance between you is con-
founding—you don't know if you can trust yourself
with the truth.

DRAWING LESSON

A step toward loss, no colors.
The glass, the leaves, the branches—all gray.

These are your words, your few words. It's a diminishment,
a necessary lesson you try

to view as a choice, a humble garden,
an arrangement of shades. The butterfly of pleasure

now a moth, an accurate line,
a plane possessing its proper shade.

You look and look, your hand disobeys,
but sometimes the pencil gets it right.

What you need to learn: To get by with less,
to represent in a new way. Represent, as if to catch

the present by evaporating into it. I was here,
say the strokes of graphite.

Your tools are simple
so you will not be distracted

by anything but the stick that is set before you—
the stick and its bent, beautiful shadow.

Cecelia Hagen

EFFECT

a riddle says x but means x + 1
this is why hands can't
make what they're made of

there's no affliction minister wrapped
in lab-coat white
crawling scuff-kneed and slow
across the linoleum
to ration doubt and be
finally *about* something

here in the nursery
in the laboratory—learning
songs in capillary time

ENLIGHTENMENT

DETROIT, MI

She is merging onto the Edsel Ford Freeway
in a car no longer made,

in a city that no longer makes it,
talking on her cellular phone, slouched to the left,

fingernails purple & red & caging the wheel,
head cocked & foot heavy.

In pursuit of a race car,
she has bought a roll of black duct tape,

has rolled three racing stripes
down the sedan's hood

as if she has been whispering with Buddha
& he said, Sister, relinquish your resistance,

your discomfort, forsake your ego.
Which she has done,

which is what it means to want
but not have

in a city stacked with desire,
to know that desire is our most ruinous trait,

the moment in the morning
when you decide to be unsatisfied & unhappy.

Our want is just one of many in a line of wants
& the line of wants is ancillary to the line of needs.

People close to you are hungry
& you have ignored it.

Crystal Williams

People close to you have lost their jobs.
Today somebody's mother has died.

Today somebody's child has been murdered.
Today some body lost sight.

& your Lumina runs.
Your Lumina runs well; Luminosity,

woman: No one is coming to save you.
There is nothing from which to be saved.

ERIC CHAVEZ IN PORTLAND

How fortunate life lies, Eric, my never-ending
birth tonight in Portland, you on rehab
with the Sacramento Rivercats,
I a mere nine rows up!

I can see the contours of your face, your brow even,
the perfect Zen in your crouch. Your precise
over-the-shoulder release. The fundamental straightness
of your back. Is that a little belly even?

Every move, every pitch, every waking
high thrust of my spirit simply yards away,
at third, all my lost dreams realized tonight

in your paced extension, gentle lean
slow gait, nervous twitch, gracious act
your glove, my heart.

EUROPE. MEMORY. SQUID PARTS. GRACE.

Whether the squid's ear resembles the diaphanous soul in ascent
or an aerial shot of Cuba,
the macabre happens and happens

Rising like a prayer from my daughter, Svetlana,
remarkable for the grace with which she moved through the insipid
stations of her teens

Educing the woman out of the girl
like scampi brought upriver by cruise ships
and served at the noisy Quinceañeras of East Los Angeles

Kind of detached from reality as evening flickers
and blogs by American males rhizomically expand in the blogspace
and Zeus hauls memory's daughter across the ocean

To an island of prosperous rental property owners
busy remembering Cuba
where Internet cafes are like churches

And churches are like monsters
once believed in and dreaded across pre-Christian Europe
now placed wistfully inside the atriums of the forgotten

as equivocal as fog, as curtains, as darkness, as closed doors.

Rodney Koeneke

EXILE OFF FOSTER

I worked past the first winter
to yesterday, when someone was stabbed
to death on the street behind me,
the first day of spring. Pistols were drawn
outside my back window, a police sniper
crouched on my neighbor's roof.
We gathered at the end of the block
for the first time, the neighbors,
like a poor man's United Nations,
smelling of beets, cocaine, and body odor:
the crack dealer, the laborer, the bartender,
the ice cream man. On this side
of the city that's yet to be in fashion,
we share two things—a history
of before here and a feeling for having settled.
In a city of trees, there are few here,
yet an abundance of birds—crows, robins,
scrub jays, finches, and hawks—that too
have resigned. They rest where we have given up,
eat from the overgrown lots.
I came here out of circumstance
and am now surrounded by organ meat,
diesel fuel, rusted radiators, dandelions,
overgrown rhododendrons covered
with dead blooms, pit bulls,
and babushka-wearing yentas
who roll their metal carts full of dinged boxes.
Soon a few desperate farmers
will put out what they've grown
on the rain-soaked dirt and gravel.
Anything to survive. Bring in some money
and vitamins. I had a family
of raccoons living in my eaves last summer.
At night, they would stare at me
from the corner of my roof.
I suppose the lesson I was meant to learn

Sid Miller

was that anyone can make a home
out of anything, so long as you're comfortable
with your lot. But the rest of us
don't seem comfortable. I toss and turn
at night. Everyone fidgets with their fingers.
And even though these are still
somewhat my people, from the Ukraine,
from Staten Island, from the far Pacific,
and from what was once all of Mexico,
something doesn't translate. Not even
my grandmother wore a babushka
and her collapsible shopping cart
was left behind years ago, cigarettes
soon after. I've hung on
to caraway seeds, sticky white rice,
the talisman that hangs next to my front door,
and a blind faith in hard work.
But I'm no longer sure that it's enough
to build a community with.
For all the interest that we might have
in each other, the only dialogue is exchanged
with loose change. Chessboards
and park benches have disappeared.
My name is never called,
my shoulder is never tapped.
And yesterday, as quickly as the man died
on the asphalt, near silence has returned.
The crow's squawk and the cars' bass
remain the only conversation.
On Sunday mornings, the bells from the church
up the road ring, but I've yet to hear
a single lullaby sung. This is a place
where even the ugly have a hard time
falling in love and only the lucky
can recognize beauty. But we're trying.
For God's sake I know that I am,
harder than I've ever done so before.
Here, the one who walked elsewhere runs.
The one who ran now flies.
The one who flew becomes holy.

And no matter who I am now
and no matter what I have done
to have a block of whores closer to me
than a good cup of black coffee.
No matter that my hands are full of slivers
and my feet are finally beginning to crack.
No matter. I want to be holy.

Sid Miller

FIRST ICE

We wake up as the darkness begins
giving way, first to an indigo

glow like laundry bluing,
phosphorescent and implausibly dense.

Shades of trees appear, then trees,
then a dreamy, scintillant

stillness unfurls as light, as landscape
under a spell. A fat sleekness

blisters and thickens the porch; in the pasture
grass blades bow down in glass sleeves.

The woods are themselves and not
themselves in their subtle glister,

the way a truly glamorous woman,
my grandmother used to say (charm bracelets rustling),

conceals every seam and trace
of her artifice, leaving pure effect.

Inside, a chef on TV makes aspic
while we wait for the forecast.

One strives for the clearest, thinnest
gel, he is saying; one wants to illuminate

one's terrine, not to thicken it!
And as he spreads his glaze, I see the soul

rise from its loaf and lay its glossy
immaterial bliss across that surface of meat &

salt with its scallion fleur-de-lis,
making it marvelous.

As the world is, today—as it was
in the beginning, that last instant

water, matter and light were one,
each distinct, not yet separate.

HEAVEN DESCRIBED

(IN THE LANGUAGE OF VISITOR'S PAMPHLETS COLLECTED FROM THE
GREYHOUND BUS STATION IN PASCO, WASHINGTON)

Hand-picked, you will enter   past
   hulks of long-silenced   waterfalls

  Through immaculate   life-sized darkness
   new varieties of lilac   and now

      Can browse   beyond the Milky Way's
      cool husks   shimmer

      And hang   among the whispers
     your offering   pure

      Among   hand-picked
  positive attitudes   forms

   We will provide   the taste
     the fruit   wildly holds

HOME, BUT HOME

The war at the bar
was on mute.
You should have heard
the songs the
jukebox played.
"It's a Family Affair."
What I can say
about the war is
I have been working
to make imaginary
enemies visionary.
You know the voices
crowding down,
I let them say what
they say. I
almost apologize.

Lucas Bernhardt

I AM PREGNANT WITH MY MOTHER'S DEATH

I grow great with her decline. When shall I be delivered?
I'll be there tomorrow, I say on the phone. She's amazed
when I arrive. *Have you met my aide?* she asks politely,
the same kind aide she's had for months.

She remembers to worry, *Do you need more blankets?*
Her radio loud in the airless house, the oxygen machine
humming and spitting as she curls on a waterproof pad.
Oooh, she moans in her sleep, *Ooh, I'm sorry. Ooooh*

thank you. I love you. I'm sorry. I love you. Ooooh.
I wake her. A gradual smile blooms. *I'm embarrassed*
she laughs, *to be such a bag of bones.* Her shrunken
skeleton kicks at my heart and inside my belly.

I'm the luckiest woman in the world, she tells me again,
I'm the luckiest woman in the world. Or else she says,
I'm the loveliest woman in the world, and doesn't notice
any difference. She touches my cheek.

This is something new in our shared lives, how she turns
so gentle. I labor hard with her. Forgiveness loosens
my stubborn bones. I am swollen with her love for me.
When shall I be delivered?

ICELANDIC CHURCH

A blind horse stands amid ash
inches from a long fall to sea.
Mostly bone, pared down to necessity,
muzzling black rock for a taste
of the grass nearby, where all day, sated,
I have watched him.

Night again is taking me like a song.
Like God, says the farmer
who is also a priest
who sleeps in the barn
during my stay.

Alive at the center of bundled hay,
the farmer and his bliss.
I cannot quite taste the mountain
behind the mountain.
And so alive in the hesitant harvest,
an unsteady cliff and its drownings.
Alive in the silent machines left rusted
and the steeple newly painted
and the horse cut from the horizon,
silhouetted in light.

 John Sibley Williams

IN MY ALTERNATE LIFE

In my alternate life
I visit *Untitled, 1949* every Sunday afternoon,
        and sometimes it hangs in a kitchen
and sometimes in a tea room in Abergavenny in Wales.
    In my alternate life I'm Chinese or Brazilian.
I'm walking a beach scattered with slate, it being Cornwall.
    Hills, hedgerows, stoats, and a prairie of flowers,
and my mother sleeps in a hammock
        and my father sketches her into a book.
        I order at the lunch counter
that was *Nighthawks* the night before.
    I sit on the stool opposite the coffee urns.
My old back feels sturdy as it did when I was eight,
    sun lights the ochre wall like terracotta jazz,
nobody bothers me, the cup never drained.
How have I forgotten the name of this piazza,
        Florence, the one with Dante
swirling his stone cloak? Walk three blocks any way
and I'll be lost.
    Sometimes swans, sometimes vultures.
Air sings oxygen like after lightning.
    Boredom slides like a dime under a cushion.
It perches like a pigeon on my head.
        And if I want to talk with someone,
there he is—young or old, American or dead or not—
    there she is. Stars anytime.
Imagination scares me less.
People are tolerant and the world is just.

IN THE MONTPARNASSE CEMETERY

Those bells mean something, you said.

At first I barely hear them, think
they are the angelus from a nearby church

but the jangling clanging
insistence of the cemetery guards

ringing hand held brass bells
before closing the high iron gates

perambulating like monks
calling the friars to prayer

or sweeping the graveyard
of mortals before the sun sets.

Darkness falls—
the call awakens souls

like Beckett,
Baudelaire and Vallejo,

summoning them for their nightly
circumambulation.

Beckett casts a fishhook eye
on the rehearsal

asks the shadows
which of the shades is Godot?

Beaudelaire escapes his
family humming verses of Poe

seeks comfort
in the arms of Jeanne Duval.

Carlos Reyes

Restive Vallejo longs only
for the snow capped Andes…

Whatever those peripatetic souls
rehearse or mumble

in prose or verse and even if
the tide of Paris traffic drowns

their crooning voices,
they will permit no living witness.

INVITATION

If I can believe in air, I can believe
in the angels of air.

Angels, come breathe with me.

Angel of abortion, angel of alchemy,
angels of barrenness & bliss,
exhale closer. Let me feel
your breath on my teeth—

I call to you, angels of embryos,
earthquakes, you of forgetfulness—

Angels of infection, cover my mouth
and nose with your mouth.

Failed inventions, tilt my head back.

Angels of prostitution and rain,
you of sheerness & sorrow,
you who take nothing,
breathe into me.

You who have cleansed your lips
with fire, I do not need to know
your faces, I do not need you
to have faces.

Angels of water insects, let me sleep
to the sound of your breathing.

You without lungs, make my chest rise—

without you my air tastes
like nothing. For you
I hold my breath.

Mary Szybist

KANSAS, 1973

My daughter nestled in a plastic seat
is nodding beside me as though in full
agreement with the logic of her dream.
I am glad for her sake the road is straight.
But the dark shimmer of a summer road
where hope and disappointment repeat
themselves all across Kansas like a dull
chorus makes the westward journey seem
itself a dream. She breathes in one great
gulp, taking deep the blazing air, and stops
my heart until she sighs the breath away.
The sun is stuck directly overhead.

I thought it all would never end. The drive,
the heat, my child beside me, the bright day
itself, that fathering time in my life.
We were going nowhere and never would,
as in a dream, or in the space between
time and memory. I saw nothing but sky
beyond the horizon of still treetops
and nothing changing down the road ahead.

LATE NAP

I take a long hot tub so that I can feel like a melon.
I dry myself off and tingle like a coral reef.
The lower sheet I pull up tight. I puff the pillows,

lie on my back, stretch out my arms and legs.
If I'm lucky, a breeze sweeps in sweet as silk.

The sleep is calm, like a coin at the bottom
of an old fortress wall that protrudes into the sea,
and the coin is almost green from the slow sloshing.

In the sleep, nobody comes after me, I don't
have to go anywhere, and I am immortal.

Peter Sears

LETTER TO THE WINDING-SHEET

After the snowfall, snowfall
jewels my hair, my church shoes

muddy the bedspread. Crazy, you
called me, not much of a lady.

Flip up the light switch.
A child, I act a child.

At night I hold a postcard:
two plums adorn

a plum tree, what we could be.
The door tight in its door frame,

the window keeps
shutting on me.

In every dream I dream
I am asleep, your fingers

closed around my wrists.
Your breathing steals the room.

You won't explain my shrinking
vision, why I never knew enough

about the topiary—every limb
is a root, every tree a tree.

LOVE ARROW

Uncovering the street and you inside me, come to me
Quite how the other's leg
Thin golden skin closing firmly change that course
Fathoms beyond, if love brave
It's hard to change good people but no oh so allow
A pattern knocking—who are you? enraptured
You're a part of the world
Opens
A rusted silo deserves a tree growing love ants
Weep for me now

NIGHT LANDING

"I am giving up the landmarks by which I might be taking my bearings."
—Antoine de Saint-Expury, pilot

The hours that counted were measured by how much sand

was left in my pocket after charming you on the beach,
by the derivative of a voice over the single engine

as I remembered
back that far. You know,
time is not what I wanted—
fly past the horizon enough
and the moon on the starboard side
cuts visibility in half every time.
Besides, it's change in atmospheric pressure that's going to get us all in
the end, anyway.

No, when hovering
over the Sargasso Sea
at night looking for landmarks,
it was etymology I wanted,

anthropological evidence it's not words that remain,
it's the space left when it quiets, the assumption of miracles.

And now it is morning
even though it is still dark,
it is morning—not last night, not last year,
it is morning.

On this earth it is always morning, somewhere.

NIGHT TRAIN

Daylight surrenders
to interior reflections
in a mottled collage
on the coach window.

My twin gazes back,
flickering as we race
through the fading
Van Gogh landscape.

Picking up speed,
we hurtle headlong
just above the track
verging on derailment.

We slam into darkness.
Plunged into silence,
I tunnel through granite,
pray for starlight.

Leah Stenson

OUR FLAG

should be green
to represent an ocean.
It should have two stars
in the first canton,
for us and navigation.
They should be of gold thread,
placed diagonally,
and not solid,
but comprised of lines.
Our flag should be silky jet.
It should have a wound,
a red river the sun must ford
when flown at half-mast.
It should have the first letter
of every alphabet ever.
When folded into a triangle
an embroidered eighth note
should rest on top
or an odd-pinnate,
with an argentine stem,
a fiery leaf, a small branch
signifying the impossible song.
Or maybe honey and blue
with a centered white pinion.
Our flag should be a veil
that makes the night weep
when it comes to dance,
a birthday present we open
upon death, the abyss we sleep
under. Our flag should hold
failure like light glinting
in a headdress of water.
It should hold the moon
as the severed head
of a white animal
and we should carry it
to hospitals and funerals,
to police stations and law offices.

Carl Adamshick

It should live, divided,
deepening its yellows
and reds, flaunting itself
in a dead gray afternoon sky.
Our flag should be seen
at weddings well after
we've departed.
It should stir in the heat
above the tables and music.
It should watch our friends
join and separate
and laugh as they go out
under the clouded night
for cold air and cigarettes.
Our flag should sing
when we cannot,
praise when we cannot,
rejoice when we cannot.
Let it be a reminder.
Let it be the aperture,
the net, the rope of dark stars.
Let it be mathematics.
Let it be the eloquence
of the process shining
on the page, a beacon
on the edge of a continent.
Let its warnings be dismissed.
Let it be insignificant
and let its insignificance shine.

Carl Adamshick

PAPER MILL

Below the basalt bluffs of Oregon City,
a steam punk circus of riveted acid skulls
spider-welded to the great skeleton of industry.
Rattling hoppers, cable-stayed stacks, iron steps up to a corrugated
     shack
where the pipe-fitters have coffee before tightening a clamp
on chip line number two.

God knows I use a lot of paper,
but there's something about a rusty red elbow
wrapped like a wound that makes me shiver back over the highway,
up to the faded blue Quonset of the American Legion's Post #5,
where Gus buys us beers.

World's first paper mill was in Bagdad, Gus tells me.
I'll be damned, another man says. If we could give up paper and oil we'd
     be all right.
We talk jobs and fishing, and how the old town is hanging on.
The young bartender with the prosthetic arm
says I should go upriver to Clackamas Park
and see those lampreys clinging to the rocks.

SOULS UNDER WATER

No longer tumbled by currents as when
long ago they were lodgers in frail bodies,
now they drift free of the flesh that was sucked
and nibbled from bones and the blood that swirled
away, its quick red streaking the deeps.

Souls mingle in the democracy of weed.
Passing through great barnacled bulkheads,
once-passengers, transparent without furs or jewels,
glide through the shiver that marks the presence
of stoker or convict, or the drunken oilman

who one night staggered to the edge of the spider-legged rig
and dreaming of his girlfriend—unusually tender
in his mind at that dizzy moment—plunged through cans
and plastic trash, into the arms of another.
Welcome, said the souls, though his ears heard nothing.

No longer sailors nor slaves, still they remember
the struck bell piercing sleep, the darkness
below decks where rats splashed in the bilges,
the wide-eyed newborn who flew over the deck rail
saved from the plantation by her mother's arm.

Oceans are thick with them: submariners floating
free of their vaults and pilots whose planes dropped
from the sky like giant guillemots but failed to surface
with a catch of fish. The careless were snatched
by sneaker waves, the joyful by cruising sharks

who dispatched them with a lunge and spat out
their splintered surfboards. Some are surprised
to find themselves here, having thought they'd ascend
to the heaven of upper airs or deep star space. But
these are the heavens, say the souls: the heavens below.

Judith Barrington

SUNDAY IS A SERIES OF HANDS

When leaves are tossed off
the roof in bags they hit
the ground like dead bodies
I put the thud in my chest
for later when I'll need it
The clouds have taken over
a monotonous haul
Your telescope is a metaphor
and anyway you can't use it here
Don't you feel it
Every broken thing just arrived
completely healed for the day
In this diorama you are
the tree and I am the same tree
We are making a stand
Miracles are rarely solvent
Every day a woman
inside the darkest shrine
rubs sacred dirt on her sorest parts
The sound she creates while praying
makes a mouse jealous
It starts to eat through the wall.

TANTALUS

The simplicity of the torture
was what always astonished him:
the receding lake of nakedness,
crispness of forbidden fruit.

Immortal, nourished on air
only his senses starved:
teeth in the apple,
hands in the clear water.

The final humiliation:
he envied Sisyphus
his boulder to lean on,
a sense of purpose.

Paul Merchant

THAT TIME AGAIN

east rain
new rain
bat out of hell rain
so dark I can't tell it's raining
step in it and don't get wet rain
what grows later
don't drink the rain
staining my glasses
eating away the tuna can I put out to measure it
b- d- t- rain
synthetic, fricative rain
rain hits the pavement so hard it rings
rain drops racing each other
sizzling rain
sweet & sour rain
rain across the street but not here
as if it's the first time rain has fallen
snake rain
steel drum rain
artisan rain
15.95 a pound rain
22 miles a gallon
rain like momma useta make
last rain
rain that can't decide which way to go
when two rain drops go through each other no one gets wet

THE BELLS OF ST. BAVO SING SCAT

Anticipating the lovers
who will soon be voices with bodies again,
the comforter on the bed fills with light
the color of sky when day puts up her feet and
slips on royal blue slippers.

Outside their window
the man on the roof dangles a dancing bear
or a baby grand or whatever
the lovers want to unhook and haul inside.

Finally, their bodies are fields
of yellow tulips fringed purple
slowly opening their fists,
the bells of St. Bavo singing scat,
fire-breathing dragons barreling out of children's books
to race through the streets of Haarlem.

Belts daddies used for beatings
stay in the loops of their pants.
Charred bodies resurrect themselves noticing
a faint smell of smoke in their sleek hair or
the tweed of their jackets, while lovers
who parted without declaring their love
feverishly lick stamps on envelopes
of yellowed love letters
or claw at blood-red wax seals.

Willa Schneberg

THE END

it was the end of something,
and so we grew sad
according to how much we'd loved it.
now, nothing
but our great variety of sadnesses
and for some
a seed of instinct suggesting
something else
may eventually begin.

THE GIANTS

Out here, all darkness, stars overhead,
I can finally see the giants. After all the years
weighing dream's fragments, I can see
how each small thing, dead bees, a girl touching
her ear, rose petals in a pool of molasses, leads
to something larger than a life, the way the eye
follows a trail of stars then sees first one
and then another constellation against the dome
of night. My giants, I can almost love them now,
their hunger, like a piece of oak in the fire
eating every piece of wood around it,
they ate everything. They left the bones scattered
on the old brown sofa, the rabbit headless
in the yard. They lumbered, light full
on their shoulders, their hair backlit and flaming,
birds and small animals fleeing as whole families
left uneaten meals behind. I know
they can't eat me. I know them as I know
that to a child I might be as large as they were,
and when they fell, the distance of their falling
was so great the blood flowed, the earth
smoldered, and when they cried their crying
filled every room with their tears, and worst of all,
when they left they always came back,
the jostling, the trestles quaking
in those days of the giants sowing their bitter gifts,
their curses, their sour blessings, their hurled
and their spilled and their shattered. What was it
that ate them, the dream they couldn't see burning
inside them, the questions they never asked,
the tree whose shadow they did not lie down under?
I can see them, all that broke them, their shirts
creased with sweat and rank oil when they climbed
into the truck's cab at dusk clutching the brown bag
and the lottery ticket. Their feet rang out,
their doors slammed, they trudged, they cried,
they gave me these stars on a dark road, the rose book
on a winter afternoon, the hooked thorns

Maxine Scates

of the climbers, the ramblers blooming over walls
and outbuildings, blooming over their graves. They
gave me everything I wouldn't have known to love
without their whine, their roar, their terrible noise.

THE UNCLES

A haunted though thoroughly logical child,
I reasoned that yes, ghosts could terrify me,
but should one take a swipe with fist
or bloody chain, the ethereal blow
would just swish through my face. But the Devil,

Lucifer himself, roasted to a dark crimson
in the fires, his two horns like thorns
of a huge rose, he frightened me down
to my groin. I hated everyone completely.
Sins stained me, stuck to my fingers and palms

like pine pitch. There were not enough decades
of Joyful or Sorrowful Mysteries to see
me clear of damnation, an eternal
pressure cooker not for rattling jars
of sweet summer peaches but for my bones

and those of the equally luckless dead
locked forever in a roil of flame. To banish
the Devil, one must banish God, too,
a quid pro quo that began my long loneliness outside

the company of angels and saints. The day
I held open the secret backdoor of my soul
and said, you two must go, silent, they stood
up from their tea in the kitchen nook
and walked past me like two severe

yet frail uncles, each with a hitch
in the step, both disgusted and shamed,
back into the pagan forest, one a whiff
of mushroom, one a brush of morning breeze.

John Morrison

[THERE IS ANOTHER LIFE]

There is another life, only we are the same sweet sinners. I held
her hand and listened when I wanted to. Outside, all the fumes
of summer. She is for the ages, gathered from sugar and knives,
beautiful cartoons of the flickering body. I never find out what my
lies are for because I'm so tired in my favorite hours.

THERE WAS A WAR

and it wasn't ours because we didn't believe in it, and we didn't have guns, but they shot at us anyway because we existed somewhere in the middle of them killing each other. what could we do but lie still and wait? we lay a long time, the grass like trees shooting into the sky. bullets like bees shooting across it. too many hours of smoke in our eyes. we were thinking: if we had guns we'd use them to get the hell out of the middle of this war.

THRESHOLD:

where mothers prop themselves, welcoming, waving, mostly waiting.
You are a frame your child passes through, the safest place to stand
when the shaking starts. You brace yourself. He draws you like this,
arms straight out, too stick-thin but the hands are perfect, splayed like
suns, long fingers, the hands he draws for you are huge. Thresh, hold:
separate the seeds, gather them back. In his pictures you all come close
to holding hands, though the fingers of your family never touch; you're
in the middle of all this reaching.

TINY ARCTIC ICE

Inhale, exhale
7 billion people breathing
Some of us in captivity
Our crops far-flung
Prison is a place where children sometimes visit
Jetted from Japan, edamame is eaten in England
Airplane air is hard to share
I breathe in what you breathe out, stranger
We send tea leaves to distant friends
Neighbors bike to build RVs at swing shift
Araucana chickens won't lay eggs in captivity
Airplanes of roses lift above Quito mountains
Cultivated from crocuses in La Mancha, saffron suffuses my rice
Status updates stack up in Prineville warehouses
Data, coal-powered and far-flung
When the fish diminish, folks find jobs in prisons
Sometimes children visit
Airplanes of microchips lift above Cascade mountains
Terminator seeds are hard to share
And the fish diminish
The roses, the tea, and the edamame, far-flung
The roses, the tea, the microchips, and you
You breathe in what I breathe out, friend

Kaia Sand

TO TAKE

I stole another woman's only scarf
and fed the calf and brushed its coat.
I tore the scarf to pieces and swore
I'd never leave the lake. The map of the lake
had a place marked by an arrow.
I buried the scarf there. I lived a little too close
to the shore and the pelicans gathered at
my back door. I emptied a bucket of fish
in the kitchen sink and opened the window wide.
Will you believe me when I say I didn't mean
to steal it? The scarf was hers, and no one there
to tell me not to take it. The pelicans
dived toward the window, but only one
made it in. The smallest one. Do you know
what happened then—how it filled its bill
with fish and flew back out the way
it came. The fish a gift for a bird that could
find enough to eat without me. The scarf
in pieces, buried near the lake with
other secrets kept nearby. I slept while the frogs
and flies sang back and forth their night time
songs. The lake was mine, the calf and pelican
safe in my keeping. I could knit another
scarf and leave it on her doorstep. I could
fill the sink with fish again. I was patient.
It was an accident, the way I took the scarf
when no one stood nearby.

VOICE OVER GUERILLAS

My body is a scar
The world starts us this way
always on the way out
of something
In my favorite movie
love is a snowball
and the screen is full
of wild dark hair
Stop and consider
the ethics of time
and give me an answer
The God particle
pastoralizes its reactor
until the trail is lost
in a riot of flowers
We all suspect everything
is an accident
on purpose
Existentially it's a toughie
But I finally did it
I met you
Isn't that enough

Sarah Bartlett

WAR AS THE CHERRY BLOSSOMS

We turn and turn and turn the soil of ourselves.

We prepare the same ancient armature,
The deception of language

is that we are beautiful, that we give and care

as the cherry blossoms
fall in the high heat of noon.

To think each moment
is new, that we are constantly beginning,
and what we do is what we have always done:

bury the dead in the vault of earth.

It's a disgrace.
We watch the season as it lets everything

rise and open.

Branches full of green. Our memory
that chain
we feel every time we walk.

WITHOUT

I drink from a glass without a rim
I stand on a ladder without rungs
I sleep in a bed with only my body,
my body from which the day's accumulations
drop away as I move in dreams
all night inside my solitude.

I ride the horse's back without a saddle
I pedal my bicycle with no hands.
No tongue, speechless, when I move into some thought
like an ice cave, slippery, forbidding.
I eat without chewing, food sliding
right past the guardian teeth. I make fires
without matches, swim without touching
a drop, see without light.
I find my way, make music
without notes, eyes closed, using both hands.

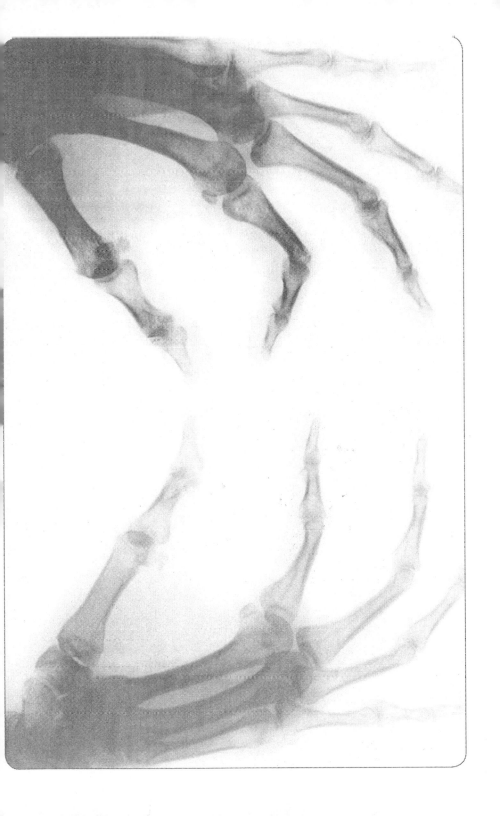

The Master's in Book Publishing at Portland State University, and Ooligan Press by extension, is a different sort of place. The students call the shots here, *learning* to publish books as they *actually* publish books. Part of our mission as a teaching institution is to teach not only our students, but our readers as well. What follows is a history of this project, *Alive at the Center*, from the graduate-student–project-manager perspective. These students follow the book along its path from acquisition to release and are intimately familiar with the book and all its personality traits. They have been kind enough to write their stories down so you, too, can be a part of the publishing process, from the student's perspective. I hope you enjoy its ups and downs, as I enjoy teaching through them, every day.

—*Abbey Gaterud, Publisher*

PACIFIC POETRY PROJECT — THE BEGINNING

The inspiration behind the Pacific Poetry Project (PPP) began in early 2010, when Ooligan Press editors expressed an interest in collaborating and publishing a new poetry collection. However, as so many regional poetry anthologies already exist, I asked the Acquisitions department (of which I was assistant manager) if I could run with a new idea, one that could stretch Ooligan's reach and potential influence beyond Oregon's borders, perhaps even America's borders.

Seattle, Washington, and Vancouver, British Columbia, are big-sister cities to Portland at heart—sharing so much culture and history, so many personalities and perspectives. I thought a literary collaboration between these Northwest artistic centers would build on this pre-existing bond.

First, the Acquisitions department hashed out a structure, creating regional editors and co-editors in order to expand the reach of the anthology. These regional editors would have their fingers on the pulse of their city, more so than Ooligan ever could. I then compiled lists of these poets and organization leaders and prepared templates for future communication with them. The list was long, as I knew some poets would be incommunicado or uninterested.

Next, I created a dozen-page marketing document, which I used to pitch the idea of PPP to the Ooligan Editorial Board. It included possible grant opportunities, social engagement ideas, and collaborations with arts organizations and government agencies. The plan brought the project's goal into focus: PPP should only contain poets who are actively involved in their local communities. This meant that the book (and therefore

Ooligan Press) would have dozens—perhaps a hundred—poets actively engaged with the book (and us) throughout the northwestern United States and British Columbia. The Editorial Board was excited by these ideas, and PPP was unanimously accepted.

Most exciting was when our publishers, Dennis and Abbey, suggested that PPP become a template for future books, serving as the first of many similar Ooligan anthologies. PPP would therefore establish Ooligan's own poetry 'brand' and series. With respect to marketing the book, it made sense to approach the endeavor as a social and cultural 'living' artifact, helping to keep it from becoming seen as "just another book on the shelf." With the help of Tony Anderson, I created a contact list of government agencies and literary organizations in the three cities, and contacted them to provide information about the publication and how it would benefit their cities. Our first time running this process, we focused on speaking of the book as a bridge between three communities.

Once accepted by Ooligan, volunteers from the Acquisitions department assisted me in contacting potential regional editors and booking all three cities. It was a difficult process but soon we confirmed the three teams of three editors for each city. We provided them with very specific guidelines and deadlines: they were given PPP's mission, scope, and marketing plan, as well as guidelines for the selection of poets within their cities. They understood what we wanted and how far we were willing to stretch our resources to help them. We knew that only collaboration could ensure the book and overall project would be a success.

After everyone was on board—all literary and government agencies were aware of the book, our social media campaign was solidified, the templates and plans were in place to ensure the participation of future editors, and all Ooligan departments were prepared—I stepped down from involvement in PPP and graduated from Portland State University.

PPP is my greatest achievement with Ooligan Press, and it was bittersweet to release my child into the world, to let it grow its own wings. I am also honored to have my own poetry within its pages, as one of the regional editors requested my work for inclusion.

—*John Sibley Williams*

FROM MANUSCRIPT TO TITLE TO COVER

Most Ooligan students manage a department or project at some point during their time in Ooligan. I signed up to be co-project manager for the Pacific Poetry Project. The previous term, I had worked with the Editing department on an initial read-through of the poems, to revise them and make queries to the authors. I was familiar with and enjoyed the content. We didn't have a title, which was necessary before the Design department could get started on a cover. As a title, Pacific Poetry Project wouldn't work. PPP was devised to be an Ooligan brand, anticipating future titles and external promotions.

In a brainstorming meeting, Abbey Gaterud (the publisher of Ooligan Press), suggested that we comb the poems for phrases that might make a fitting title. With highlighter in hand, that's exactly what I did. I went through all three regions (Portland, Seattle, and Vancouver): about 160 poems total. I made a list of forty phrases extracted from lines of the poems. Even taken completely out of context, some of these title contenders stood up surprisingly well. I knew I had too many possible titles to ever bring to a meeting, so I narrowed my forty down to twenty and threw them in a mass Ooligan survey. This way, my fellow students could help me determine a title.

The goal of developing the survey was to get students to read the poems and reflect on consistent themes and marketing ideas for the anthology. The question, "What should we avoid when designing the cover?" struck a chord. The consensus was that the press did not want any Pacific Northwest clichés (rain, rural settings, too much nature, abundance of the color green, etc.).

The poems ranged in setting. Many were urban, plenty were natural, but the majority shared a sense of melancholy and disillusionment. The most prevalent themes were light and darkness—both figuratively and literally. My co-manager (and now dear friend, thanks to the PPP project), Rachel Pass, helped me consolidate the responses. We then did some research, gabbed and honed our own ideas, and constructed a design brief. We sent it to the Design department so they could start thinking about covers. Still, they wouldn't have all the components necessary to build a solid cover until we had a solid title.

All Ooligan votes take place at Executive meetings, where everyone in the press has a chance to be heard. I'd prepared some notes for orchestrating a discussion regarding PPP's title. Based on feedback within the surveys and my own instincts, I'd narrowed the list down to ten possibilities. I put nine up on the dry erase board at the meeting, including one or two originals not taken from within lines of the poems, but suggested by students. I didn't realize how invested I was in the prosperity of this project until I heard myself talking about it.

I led the group down the list and we crossed out titles one by one. We examined the pros and cons of each contender: how it would or would not uphold the integrity of each poem and the collection as a whole; how it would appeal to or turn off readers; how it would represent the press and the three regions from which the poems hail; what would pop up online if someone did a search using the title's key words (a student sat with a laptop typing each possible title into Google, to ensure that nothing too raunchy would surface if we titled our anthology *Know the Trapdoors* or *Nothing Holds Like I Do*—real examples). The discussion was fun, and it got pretty intense, as Ooligan consists of passionate people with various tastes, experiences, and perspectives to offer.

Overall, students made it clear they did not want a title with an "I" in it, or anything too cryptic or interpretive, or anything quaint and romantic that could ever be the title to a country western song. An hour later, our list had shrunk to two, but everyone seemed to be a bit over those two prospects. Compromising is one thing, but settling is another. I knew I couldn't make all Ooliganites happy with one title, but I couldn't accept that everyone would leave the meeting uninspired. That's when I pulled out the kicker. Saying casually, "Oh look, I forgot this one—the tenth contender…" I wrote, *Alive at the Center* on the board. The room may as well have shaken with the shift in enthusiasm. We were rejuvenated and within seconds, the time it took me to count the "yays" and "nays," it was all over. All but two hands out of a fifty were up in the final vote for this title contender.

The front cover for our anthology was inspired by this title and designed by one of Ooligan's talented students, J. Adam Collins. By restricting the color, there is a subliminal feeling of harmony between the image and the semantics of the title. The eye-catching, haunting image of the skeletal fingers and the vibrant bird in flight creates a provocative intrigue. Heavy with symbolism, the fingers signify the life as well as the dormant death within us.

The x-ray reference evokes the role of the machine, which speaks to our modern world. We don't actually see the machine, just the result—that is, our bones. In this way the hands are pure, organic, and relatable. In context with the hands, the image of the bird is nature reinvented, and the movement captured is a visceral one. The image also thrives within the tension between the forms. Is this bird about to be crushed or cradled? Perhaps the most accurate answer is, "both," as people will see what they want to see, and either perception sparks an emotional reaction.

With all due respect, I find the majority of poetry anthologies have forgettable covers, though the content may be anything but. Ooligan needed this unforgettable cover to represent the words within. The only risk would have been *not taking a risk* on this maverick design. I believe it will command attention on any bookshelf.

—*Amber May*

FROM PERMISSIONS TO GALLEYS AND BEYOND

Like Amber, I came to work on the Pacific Poetry Project in January of 2012, just before the title was chosen and the cover was designed. I was scared stiff when I volunteered for the job. I had no idea how I would juggle a management role at the press while working and taking classes. However, within a week of starting the job, I learned two invaluable things:

1. All Ooligonians are in the same busy position, so I had no right to whine.
2. The best way to get your feet wet at the press is to dive in headfirst and start swimming.

At Ooligan, this means braving a steady current of meetings, e-mails, and friendly debates; all the while gauging the pull of Ooligan's separate book projects—each project acts as a separate moon and creates complicated tides. At first this was overwhelming. But once I became familiar with the work, I saw that I wouldn't sink if I reached out for help when the current got too strong. Everyone at Ooligan is ready and willing to help.

As soon as I was comfortable in my position, I realized what an incredible opportunity I had been handed. The Pacific Poetry Project is a huge risk with a huge heart. In its mission to seek out and connect the myriad poets of the Northwest's three largest cities in a borderless artistic community, it has tested the considerable abilities of all the departments in our press community.

Many challenging tasks made the Pacific Poetry Project a success. We have had to keep an extensive database for permissions, documenting whether or not we could legally print the more than 200 poems submitted by over 160 poets. We designed and created four separate covers—one for the anthology, and three equally stunning covers for the individual city editions. Marketing and promoting these beautiful books involved everything from a grass-roots reading series to an extensive online presence; a conference with national sales representatives assured that we will have booksellers throughout and beyond the Northwest on board when the book goes live.

There have been struggles along the way. Some production deadlines flew by unmet, some technology demons crept up and ate the occasional document, and some debates grew too heated. But that is the way of any press. I'm proud to say that throughout the past two and a half years since the book's conception, no problem has arisen that the press hasn't been able to band together to solve.

It is now July of 2012. Jonathan Stark and I are the project's current co-managers. We are in the privileged position of looking back and admiring the incredible amount of work that has been done to bring *Alive at the Center*, the first installment of the Pacific Poetry Project series, to fruition.

There is, however, no treading water at Ooligan as there is always more work to be done. Next month we will send out copies for review and our Editing department will apply for *Alive at the Center*'s official library listing from the Library of Congress. In light of all of this we want to thank everyone within and outside of the press who has had a hand in this project to date, as well as those who will step in to plan and execute the separate city launches. Thank you, for making sure this book finds its well-deserved community of readers, who will love it as much as we do.

—*Rachel Pass*

THE PROJECT NEVER ENDS

My first involvement in the Pacific Poetry Project was to suggest a title to Amber May: *Stealing Home Again*. Thankfully, despite the complicated metaphor which informed my suggestion, it wasn't chosen. Heck, I voted for *Alive at the Center*. That could have marked the extent of my involvement with the project, but a term later Amber retired from being its project manager and a need for someone to take her spot was created. I tentatively signed up.

I say tentative not because I was wary of the project. Actually, the chance to work on a poetry anthology seemed a very unique one, and exciting. Certainly it was outside of the norm for your usual graduate school work. I was more concerned with my lack of experience in the press. This was only my second term. The Pacific Poetry Project already had a rich and tumultuous history behind it, spanning back to 2010. I was introduced to this history by Rachel Pass in a flurry of explanations, Google documents, and meetings with people who seemed to genuinely believe I knew the answers to their questions. Continuing Rachel's metaphor, I questioned my ability to be able to navigate these choppy waters. When it comes to water, I am, at best, a decent doggy-paddler.

So I doggy-paddled. And I tried to keep the shoreline in sight.

I won't lie—working on *Alive at the Center* was overwhelming at times. It was also exhilarating. Being counted on to bring something to success can show you a determination you didn't know you had. In the course of my work I learned some valuable lessons about project management. Always smile. Approach every person you work with as if they were a close friend and soon they will be. Tackle every problem with a full heart and an open mind. Remember that you are not the first person to paddle these waters, nor will you be the last. After all...

...the project never ends.

When we sweat and bleed over something, a piece of ourselves is imprinted on it. In this way, it is hard for me to move on from *Alive at the Center,* because there's a bit of me in its pages. But it is now time to pass the project on once again—this time to you, the reader.

One of the wonderful things about poetry is that it is not a static art form. It does not tell one story set in stone, but rather tells as many stories as exist in our hearts. Poetry is an active language, which asks us to interact with its every word and carefully arranged syllables. The readers will be the new project managers of *Alive at the Center,* reinterpreting it every time they browse its pages, adding their own thoughts and imprinting their own meaning on each poem. In doing this, readers will become a part of the project's history, expanding it far beyond the horizon that everyone who worked on it swam towards. Take this project, own it, and approach it with heart and smiles.

And happy paddling.

—*Jonathan Stark*

If you enjoyed reading about this book's story, check out the Start to Finish project on the Ooligan Press website: www.ooliganpress.pdx.edu

PORTLAND

Andrew Michael Roberts is the author of *something has to happen next*, which was awarded the Iowa Poetry Prize. He has two chapbooks: *Dear Wild Abandon* and *Give Up*, and is the recipient of a national chapbook fellowship from the Poetry Society of America and a distinguished teaching award from the University of Massachusetts Amherst. A cyclist and runner, he lives in Portland with his wife Sarah, and is currently a nursing student at Oregon Health and Science University.

Camille Rankine is the author of *Slow Dance with Trip Wire*, selected by Cornelius Eady for the Poetry Society of America's 2010 New York Chapbook Fellowship. She was also the recipient of a 2010 "Discovery"/ Boston Review Poetry Prize. Her poetry has been published in several magazines and journals, including *American Poet, Boston Review,* and *O, The Oprah Magazine*. She is Assistant Director of the Graduate Program in Creative Writing at Manhattanville College.

Carl Adamshick is the author of the poetry collection *Curses and Wishes*, which won the Stafford/Hall Award for Poetry at the 2012 Oregon Book Awards. He is also the recipient of an Oregon Literary Fellowship from Literary Arts and the 2010 winner of the Walt Whitman Award and the William Stafford poet-in-residence at Lewis & Clark College. His work has been published in *Harvard Review, American Poetry Review,* and *Narrative,* among others. Carl currently lives in Portland, where he co-founded and runs Tavern Books.

Carlos Reyes is a prolific poet and well-known translator. He has published four collections of his own poetry including his most recent title, *Pomegranate, Sister of the Heart* (2012), as well as numerous translations. His honors include the receipt of a Heinrich Boll Fellowship, the Ethel Fortner Award from St. Andrews College, and a poet-in-residence position at Joshua Tree National Park. He currently lives in Portland, where he is the publisher and editor of Trask House Books, Inc.

Cecelia Hagen is the author of *Entering* (Airlie Press, 2011) and two chapbooks, *Fringe Living* (26 Books Press) and *Among Others* (Traprock Books). Her poetry, reviews, and nonfiction have been published by *Rolling Stone, Prairie Schooner, Poet & Critic,* and many other publications. Her work also is, or will be included, in public art projects at the Kaiser Medical Center in Hillsboro, Oregon, Lane Community College, and downtown Eugene.

Clemens Starck is the author of five poetry books: *Journeyman's Wages, Studying Russian on Company Time, China Basin, Traveling Incognito,* and *Rembrandt, Chainsaw.* He has received the Oregon Book Award as well as the William Stafford Memorial Poetry Award from the Pacific Northwest Booksellers Association. He lives in the country outside of Dallas, Oregon, in the Willamette Valley.

Crystal Williams is the author of three collections of poems, most recently *Troubled Tongues,* winner of the 2009 Naomi Long Madgett Poetry Award. She has just completed a fourth collection of poems, titled *Detroit as Barn.* Widely anthologized, her poems also appear in journals and publications such as *The American Poetry Review, The Northwest Review,* and *Ms.* magazine, among others. Crystal holds an MFA from Cornell University, and has received fellowships and grants from The MacDowell Arts Colony, Literary Arts, the Oregon Arts Commission, and Money for Women/Barbara Deming Memorial Fund. She is dean of institutional diversity and associate professor of creative writing at Reed College.

Dan Raphael is a poet, performer, editor, reading arranger, and author of more than thirteen poetry collections. He has also collaborated with jazz saxophonist Rich Halley and drummer Carson Halley to create a performance CD. Dan has performed more than 250 times, in places like Wordstock, Bumbershoot, Powell's Books, Eastern Oregon University, Portland Jazz Festival, and other Portland venues. He edited NRG *Magazine* for seventeen years, and has hosted Poetland in the past.

Daneen Bergland's poems have appeared in various journals and magazines, including *Propeller, The Denver Quarterly,* and *Poet Lore.* Daneen has received a fellowship from Oregon Literary Arts, a Pushcart Prize nomination, and awards from the Academy of American Poets.

David Biespiel is the president of the Attic Institute, a haven for writers in Portland. He is the author of four books of poetry, including *The Book of Men and Women, Wild Civility, Pilgrims & Beggars,* and *Shattering Air,* as well as a book on creativity, *Every Writer Has a Thousand Faces.*

Dean Gorman lives in Portland, where he plays in the bands The Tumblers and Sweet William's Ghost. He graduated from the Vermont College MFA program and co-founded Pilot Books and Magazine. His work has appeared in *Gulf Coast, The Indiana Review,* and *Forklift Ohio,* among others.

Donna Henderson's poems have appeared widely in magazines and anthologies, and earned her two Pushcart Prize nominations. *The Eddy Fence* is her first full-length poetry collection. She is a founding member of the poetry and classical piano performance trio Tonepoem, based at Western Oregon University, and also a founding member of Airlie Press. Donna maintains a psychotherapy practice in Monmouth, Oregon, and teaches creative writing at Willamette University.

Emily Kendal Frey is the author of the full-length poetry collection *The Grief Performance* (Cleveland State University Poetry Center, 2011), which was selected for the Cleveland State Poetry Center's 2010 First Book Prize. She also won the Poetry Society of America's 2012 Norma Farber First Book Award. Emily's poetry also appears in other publications including *Octopus* and *The Oregonian*, and she's the author of numerous chapbooks. Emily received an MFA from Emerson College, and currently lives in Portland.

Floyd Skloot's seventeen books include the poetry collections *The Snow's Music* (LSU Press, 2008) and *Selected Poems: 1970–2005* (Tupelo Press, 2008), winner of a Pacific Northwest Book Award. He has won three Pushcart Prizes, and his work has been included twice each in *The Best American Essays*, *Best American Science Writing*, *Best Spiritual Writing*, and *Best Food Writing* anthologies.

Henry Hughes is the author of three poetry collections: *Men Holding Eggs* (winner of the 2004 Oregon Book Award), *Moist Meridian* (2011), and *Shutter Lines* (2012). He is the editor of the anthology, *The Art of Angling: Poems About Fishing*, and his commentary on new poetry appears regularly in *Harvard Review*.

Jennifer Richter's book *Threshold* has been a national bestseller, and her work has appeared in *Poetry*, *Poetry Northwest*, and *The Missouri Review*, among others. She was awarded a Wallace Stegner Fellowship and Jones Lectureship in Poetry by Stanford University, where she taught in the Creative Writing Program for four years. Jennifer teaches for Stanford's Online Writer's Studio and as Visiting Poet in Oregon State University's MFA Program; she lives in Corvallis, Oregon, with her children and her husband, novelist Keith Scribner.

Jerry Harp is the author of three books of poetry: *Creature* (Salt Publishing, 2003), *Gatherings* (Ashland Poetry Press, 2004), and *Urban Flowers, Concrete Plains* (Salt Publishing, 2006). He co-edited *A Poetry*

Criticism Reader with Jan Wiessmiler. His essays and reviews appear regularly in *Pleiades*. He teaches at Lewis & Clark College.

Jesse Lichtenstein is a journalist, poet, screenwriter, and teacher. He is a founder and co-director of the Loggernaut Reading Series and currently spends most of his time in Oregon.

Though now pursuing a PhD in Creative Writing at the University of Denver, **Jesse Morse** will always consider the Northwest one of his three homes. He's had various pieces published in various places (like *Bombay Gin* and *Fiction Brigade*), and Portland-based c_l Press put out a chapbook called *Rotations*, with a lot more Eric Chavez poems of a completely different nature. Jesse spends much of his time playing outdoors with his labradane, Hank.

John Morrison's book, *Heaven of the Moment*, won the Rhea & Seymour Gorsline Poetry Competition. He received his MFA from the University of Alabama. John's poetry has appeared in numerous national journals including the *Cimarron Review*, *Poet Lore*, and *Poetry East*, among others. John has taught poetry at the University of Alabama, Washington State University, and in the Literary Arts Writers in the Schools program where he served as director from 2006–2009. He is currently an Adjunct Fellow at the Attic Institute.

John Sibley Williams is the author of six chapbooks and winner of the HEART Poetry Award. He has served as an acquisitions manager at Ooligan Press, been an agent and publicist, and holds an MFA in Creative Writing and MA in Book Publishing. A few previous publishing credits include: *Inkwell*, *Bryant Literary Review*, *Cream City Review*, *The Chaffin Journal*, *The Evansville Review*, RHINO, *Rosebud*, *Ellipsis*, *Flint Hills Review*, and various other fiction and poetry anthologies.

Judith Barrington is the author of three poetry collections, most recently *Horses and the Human Soul*, selected by Oregon's State Library for "150 Books for the Sesquicentennial." She has also recently published two poetry chapbooks, including the Robin Becker Award-winning, *Lost Lands*. Her *Lifesaving: A Memoir* was winner of the Lambda Literary Award. Her other awards include The Dulwich International Poetry Prize and The Stuart Holbrook Award from Literary Arts. She teaches literary memoir in the University of Alaska's MFA program and lives in Oregon.

Kaia Sand is the author of the book *Remember to Wave* (Tinfish Press, 2010)—also the name of a walk Sand leads in North Portland. Both the book and walking tour investigate political history and current goings-on. She is also the author of the poetry collection *interval* (Edge Books, 2004), and co-author with Jules Boykoff of *Landscapes of Dissent* (Palm Press, 2008). She participates in the Dusie Kollektiv, recently creating a broadside of her embroidered 8 ft. drop cloth poem. She is a member of PEN American Center and teaches at Pacific University.

Kathleen Halme grew up in Wakefield, a post-mining and logging town in Michigan's upper peninsula, but now lives in Portland. She completed her MFA in Creative Writing at the University of Michigan, where her work was awarded the Hopwood Creative Writing Award. Her honors include a National Endowment for the Arts fellowship in poetry, a National Endowment for the Humanities fellowship in anthropology, and an Oregon Literary Fellowship. Her poems have appeared widely in journals, including *Poetry, Ploughshares*, and *Virginia Quarterly Review,* among others. Her three books of poetry are: *Every Substance Clothed* (winner of the University of Georgia Press Contemporary Poetry Series and the Balcones Poetry Prize), *Equipoise,* and *Drift and Pulse.*

Kirsten Rian is a widely published essayist and poet, with work appearing in magazines, international literary journals, and anthologies. She is the author of three books, including the forthcoming *Chord,* to be released in early 2013 through Wordcraft. She co-authored the now-sold-out Northwest anthology, *Walking Bridges Using Poetry as a Compass* (Urban Adventure Press). Her anthology of Sierra Leonean poetry, *Kalashnikov in the Sun* (Pika Press), was released in 2010; this collection is in every classroom in Sierra Leone, and is used as a textbook on discussing and processing war at the Kroc Institute for International Peace Studies Institute of the University of Notre Dame.

Leah Stenson earned an MA in English Literature in 1971, and went on to do editorial work for the Soka Gakkai, serve as Managing Director of the Oregon Peace Institute for three years, actively support various nonprofit organizations, and publish multiple chapbooks. Leah has co-authored an English textbook as well as articles and book reviews, some of which have appeared in *The Oregonian, The World Tribune,* and *School Library Journal.* Her poetry has appeared in *Oregon Literary Review, Northwest Women's Journal,* and *Verseweavers,* among others.

Lex Runciman teaches at Linfield Collge, where the English department offers degrees in literature and in creative writing. This shows how the culture has changed: when Lex was an undergraduate (at a good school in California), the curriculum offered a single course in creative writing—which he took as a freshman. When, at the end of the term, Lex said to the teacher, "That was fun, I want to do more of it," the response he heard was "you can't—we have one course called Imaginative Writing, and you've just finished it."

Lisa Steinman, Kenan Professor of English & Humanities at Reed College, is the author of three books about poetry including *Invitation to Poetry* (Blackwell), four volumes of poetry, and a poetry chapbook. Winner of the Oregon Book Award for *All That Comes to Light*, Lisa's work has also received recognition from the National Endowment for the Arts, the National Endowment for the Humanities, and the Rockeller Foundation, among others. Her poems have appeared in such journals as *Notre Dame Review, Chariton Review, Chicago Review*, and *Michigan Quarterly*, among others. She also co-edits the poetry magazine *Hubbub*.

Lucas Bernhardt is a freelance writer and editor who also teaches writing at Portland State University. He earned MA degrees in English Literature and in Writing from PSU, and an MFA from the Iowa Writers' Workshop. He is the managing editor of *Propeller* magazine, and his own work has appeared in a number of magazines.

Mary Szybist grew up in Pennsylvania, and earned her MFA from the Iowa Writers' Workshop, where she was also a Teaching-Writing Fellow. Mary's poetry has appeared in *Denver Quarterly, The Iowa Review*, and *Poetry*, among others. She received a fellowship from the National Endowment for the Arts, and is one of two recipients of the 2009 Witter Bynner Award. Her collection of poems, *Granted* (Alice James Books, 2003) won the 2003 Beatrice Hawley Award from Alice James Books and the 2004 Great Lakes Colleges Association New Writers Award. Mary is currently an assistant professor of English at Lewis & Clark College.

About becoming a poet, **Maxine Scates** says, "I'm not sure that I really had a choice; poetry was the form that called to me as a way of making sense of the world, and at eighteen or nineteen it was the only thing anyone had ever told me I was good at—though now I suspect good meant promising! In its way, 'The Giants' was a given poem—once I'd found the metaphor, the poem flowed easily (which is not always the case) but I recall particular pleasure in writing this poem."

Paul Merchant is a poet, translator, and the William Stafford Archivist at Lewis & Clark College. He taught for many years at Warwick University before moving to Oregon. His recent translations from modern Greek include *Monochords* by Yannis Ritsos, published in 2007 by Trask House Press, and *Twelve Poems about Cavafy*, published by Tavern Books in 2010.

Oregon's sixth Poet Laureate, **Paulann Petersen**, has published five full-length books of poetry, most recently *The Voluptuary* (Lost Horse Press). Her poems have appeared in many journals and anthologies, including *Poetry*, *The New Republic*, and *Prairie Schooner*, among others. A former Stegner Fellow at Stanford University and the recipient of the 2006 Holbrook Award from Oregon Literary Arts, she serves on the board of Friends of William Stafford, organizing the January Stafford Birthday Events.

Penelope Scambly Schott is the author of five chapbooks and eight full-length books of poetry. Her verse biography, *A is for Anne: Mistress Hutchinson Disturbs the Commonwealth*, received the 2008 Oregon Book Award for Poetry. Her most recent book, *Crow Mercies* (2010), was awarded the Sarah Lantz Memorial Poetry Prize from Calyx Press. Penelope lives in Portland and teaches an annual poetry workshop in Dufur, Oregon.

Peter Sears graduated from Yale University and the Iowa Writers' Workshop. He won the 1999 Peregrine Smith Poetry Competition and the 2000 Western States Poetry Prize for his book, *The Brink*. He has published several full length collections and his work can also be found in a variety of magazines and literary journals, as well as on the radio series, *The Writer's Almanac*. His most recent full-length book is titled *Green Diver*. Sears founded and manages the Oregon Literary Coalition and co-founded the nonprofit organization Friends of William Stafford.

Robert Duncan Gray—who authored the introduction to the *Alive at the Center* anthology—is an Englishman who grew up in the Black Forest of southwestern Germany. He studied art at the University of California, Santa Barbara, and currently lives and works in Portland. He is an editor and webmaster for HOUSEFIRE and the author of CABBAGE LAN-GUAGE (forthcoming on HOUSEFIRE, 2012) and *cloud / moustache* (NAP, 2012). Rob works on writing, reading, performing, photography, painting, drawing, and music.

Rodney Koeneke is the author of the poetry collections *Musee Mechanique* (BlazeVOX, 2006) and *Rouge State* (Pavement Saw, 2002), and numerous chapbooks. His writing has appeared in *Aufgabe, The Nation,* and ZYZZYVA, among others. Since moving to Portland in 2006, he's written a poetry-focused blog, *Modern Americans* and reviewed nearly 300 books of (mostly contemporary) poetry on Goodreads. An essay on the poet Hannah Weiner can be found online at the University of Buffalo's Electronic Poetry Center.

Sarah Bartlett lives in Portland, and reads poetry for *Tin House*. She received a MFA from Emerson College. Her chapbook *A Mule-Shaped Cloud* (Horse Less Press), co-authored with Chris Tonelli, came out in 2008. Her work has appeared in a number of literary journals including *Diagram, Past Simple, Bat,* and *Rhino*, among others.

Scot Siegel's most recent book of poetry is *Thousands Flee California Wildflowers* (Salmon Poetry, 2012), and his most recent work appears in *American Poetry Journal, High Desert Journal,* and *Open Spaces: Voices of the Northwest* (University of Washington Press, 2011). Siegel lives near Portland, where he works as a town-planning consultant and serves on the board of the Friends of William Stafford. He edits *Untitled Country Review,* an online journal of poetry and visual art.

Sid Miller, the founding editor of the poetry journal *Burnside Review* and a Pushcart Prize nominee, has seen wide publication of his work. He has three full-length poetry collections to his name, his chapbook *Quietly Waiting* was published in 2004 by White Heron Press, and his work has also appeared in other publications including *The Oregonian, Portland Review,* and *High Desert Journal*. He lives in Portland.

Susan Denning is a writer who lives in Portland. She edited the online magazine *Caffeine Destiny* for thirteen years.

W. Vandoren Wheeler's poems have appeared in *Swink, H_ngM_n,* and *Bat City Review,* among others. He earned an MFA from Warren Wilson, and edited Marylhurst University's *M Review* for two years. He teaches composition, creative writing, and literature at Portland Community College. His manuscript, *The Accidentalist,* won the 2012 Dorothy Brunsman Prize.

Willa Schneberg is the author of three poetry collections: *Box Poems; In The Margins of the World* (winner of the Oregon Book Award for Poetry);

and *Storytelling in Cambodia*. Among the publications and anthologies in which her poems have appeared are: *American Poetry Review; The Year's Best Fantasy and Horror* (St. Martin's Press); and *I Go the Ruined Place: Contemporary Poems in Defense of Global Human Rights* (Lost Horse Press). In fall of 2012, her interdisciplinary exhibit entitled "The Books of Esther" was on view at the Oregon Jewish Museum.

All poems are published with permission of the poet, in addition to the permission of any previous publisher, as cited below.

PORTLAND

"Accidents of Trees," Daneen Bergland. Reprinted with permission from *Hayden's Ferry Review,* Issue 41 (Fall/Winter 2007–08).

"A Man Who Was Afraid of Language," Jerry Harp Reprinted. with permission from *Notre Dame Review: The First Ten Years,* University of Notre Dame Press, 2009, and Creature, Cambridge, UK: Salt Publishing, 2003. First published in *Notre Dame Review* 6 (Summer 1998).

"Annunciation: Eve to Ave," Mary Szybist. From *Incarnadine.* Copyright © 2012 by Mary Szybist. Reprinted with the permission of The Permissions Company, Inc. on behalf of Graywolf Press, Minneapolis, Minnesota, www.graywolfpress.org. First appeared in *The Iowa Review.*

"Appetite," Paulann Petersen. Reprinted with permission from *The Wild Awake,* Confluence Press, 2002, and *Poetry* 178, no. 4 (July 2001).

"Avulsion" Kathleen Halme. From *Equipoise.* Copyright © 1998 by Kathleen Halme. Reprinted with permission of The Permissions Company, Inc. on behalf of Sarabande Books, Inc. www.sarabandebooks.org

"Bloodline," Paulann Petersen. Reprinted with permission from *The Voluptuary.* Sandpoint, ID: Lost Horse Press, 2010.

"Dismantling," Clemens Starck. Reprinted with permission from *Journeyman's Wages.* Ashland, OR: Story Line Press, 1995.

"Distant Friends," Lisa Steinman. Reprinted with permission from *Carslaw's Sequences.* University of Tampa Press, 2003.

"Don't Ask, Don't Tell," Scot Siegel. Reprinted with permission from *Thousands Flee California Wildflowers.* Cliffs of Moher, County Clare, Ireland: Salmon Poetry, 2012.

"Drawing Lesson," Cecelia Hagen. Reprinted with permission from *Caffeine Destiny,* www.caffeinedestiny.com.

"Enlightenment," Crystal Williams. Forthcoming in *Angles of Ascent: A Norton Anthology of Contemporary African American Poetry.* New York: W.W. Norton, 2013. Reprinted with permission from *Connotation Press: An Online Artifact* (April 2010).

"First Ice," Donna Henderson. Reprinted with permission from *The Eddy Fence,* Monmouth, OR: Airlie Press, 2009, and *A Fine Madness* 9 (2004).

"Heaven Described," Mary Szybist. Copyright © 2012 by Mary Szybist. Reprinted with the permission of The Permissions Company, Inc. on behalf of the author. First appeared in *Mare Nostrum.*

"I am pregnant with my mother's death," Penelope Scambly Schott. Reprinted with permission from *Six Lips.* Woodstock, NY: Mayapple Press, 2009.

"Icelandic Church," John Sibley Williams. Reprinted with permission from *From Colder Climates.* Rocklin, CA: Folded Word, 2012.

"In My Alternate Life," Lex Runciman. Reprinted with permission from *Starting from Anywhere.* County Clare, Ireland: Salmon Poetry, 2009.

"In the Montparnasse Cemetery," Carlos Reyes. Reprinted with permission from *Pomegranate, Sister of the Heart.* Sandpoint, IL. Lost Horse Press, 2012.

"Invitation," Mary Szybist. From *Incarnadine.* Copyright © 2012 by Mary Szybist. Reprinted with the permission of The Permissions Company, Inc. on behalf of Graywolf Press, Minneapolis, Minnesota, www.graywolfpress.org. First appeared in *Electronic Poetry Review.*

"Kansas, 1973," Floyd Skloot. Reprinted with permission from *Selected Poems: 1970–2005.* North Adams, MA: Tupelo Press, 2008.

"Late Nap," Peter Sears. Reprinted with permission from *Luge.* Corvallis, OR: Cloudbank, 2009

"Night Landing," Kirsten Rian. Reprinted with permission from *Broad River Review* (2011).

"Night Train," Leah Stenson. Reprinted with permission from *Heavenly Body.* Georgetown, KY: Finishing Line Press, 2011.

"Paper Mill," Henry Hughes. Reprinted with permission from *basalt* 6, no. 1 (Spring 2011).

"Souls Under Water," Judith Barrington. Reprinted with permission from *Postcard from the Bottom of the Sea.* Portland, OR: The Eighth Mountain Press, 2008.

"Tantalus," Paul Merchant. Reprinted with permission from *Stones.* Exeter, UK: Rougemont Press, 1973.

"That Time Again," Dan Raphael. Reprinted with permission from *Windfall: A Journal of Poetry of Place* (Spring 2007) and *The State I'm In.* Nine Muses, 2007.

"The Bells of St. Bavo Sing Scat," Willa Schneberg. Reprinted with permission from *Storytelling in Cambodia.* Corvallis, OR: Calyx Books, 2006.

"The Giants," Maxine Scates.
Reprinted with permission from
Undone. Kalamazoo, MI: Western
Michigan University (New Issues
Poetry & Prose), 2011.

"There was a war, the end," Andrew
Michael Roberts. Reprinted with
permission from *New Ohio Review* 3
(Spring 2008).

"Threshold:," Jennifer Richter.
Reprinted with permission from
Threshold. Southern Illinois University
Press, 2010.

"Without," Cecelia Hagen. Reprinted
with permission from *Caffeine Destiny*,
www.caffeinedestiny.com (website
discontinued December 2012).

ACKNOWLEDGEMENTS

OOLIGAN
PRESS

Ooligan Press takes its name from a Native American word for the common smelt or candlefish. Ooligan is a general trade press rooted in the rich literary life of Portland and the Department of English at Portland State University. Ooligan is staffed by students pursuing master's degrees in an apprenticeship program under the guidance of a core faculty of publishing professionals.

Acquisitions
Tony Anderson
J. Adam Collins
John Sibley Williams

Permissions
Katie Allen
Heather Frazier
Tara Lehmann
Jonathan Stark
Kristen Svenson

Editors
Katie Allen
Kylie Byrd
Gino Cerruti
Heather Frazier
Rachel Hanson
Rebekah Hunt
Tiah Lindner
Amber May
Isaac Mayo
Anne Paulsen
Ashley Rogers
Jonathan Stark
Kristen Svenson
Jennifer Tibbett
Amreen Ukani
Amanda Winterroth

Cover Design
J. Adam Collins

Interior Design
Poppy Milliken
Lorna Nakell

Miscellaneous Design
Brandon Freels
Mandi Russell
Kelsey Yocum

Online materials
Kate Burkett

E-book Design
Kai Belladone
Anna Smith

Logo Design
Tristen Jackman
Lisa Shaffer

Marketing & Sales
Emily Gravlin
Kristin Howe
Kathryn Ostendorff

Project Management
J. Adam Collins
Joel Eisenhower
Amber May
Tina Morgan
Kathryn Ostendorff
Rachel Pass
Jessica Snavlin
Jonathan Stark
John Sibley Williams

OOLIGAN
P R E S S

369 Neuberger Hall
724 SW Harrison Street
Portland, Oregon 97201
Phone: 503.725.9748 | Fax: 503.725.3561
ooligan@ooliganpress.pdx.edu | ooligan.pdx.edu

Ooligan Press is a general trade publisher rooted in the rich literary tradition of the Pacific Northwest. A region widely recognized for its unique and innovative sensibilities, this small corner of America is one of the most diverse in the United States, comprising urban centers, small towns, and wilderness areas. Its residents range from ranchers, loggers, and small business owners to scientists, inventors, and corporate executives. From this wealth of culture, Ooligan Press aspires to discover works that reflect the values and attitudes that inspire so many to call the Northwest their home.

Founded in 2001, Ooligan is a teaching press dedicated to the art and craft of publishing. Affiliated with Portland State University, the press is staffed by students pursuing master's degrees in an apprenticeship program under the guidance of a core faculty of publishing professionals.

Ordering information:

Individual Sales: All Ooligan Press titles are available through your local bookstore, and we encourage supporting independent booksellers. Please contact your local bookstore, or purchase online through Powell's, Indiebound, or Amazon.

Retail Sales: Ooligan books are distributed to the trade through Ingram Publisher Services. Booksellers and businesses that wish to stock Ooligan titles may order directly from IPS at (866) 400-5351 or customerservice@ingrampublisherservices.com.

Educational and Library Sales: We sell directly to educators and libraries that do not have an established relationship with IPS. For pricing, or to place an order, please contact us at operations@ooliganpress.pdx.edu.

Close Is Fine

**a short story collection
by Eliot Treichel**

fiction | 168 pages | $14.95
5½" × 8½" | softcover | ISBN: 978-1-932010-45-9

OOLIGAN
PRESS

Like a Polaroid snapshot, this finely wrought collection of short stories gives us a brief glimpse into the quirky and complex lives of rural town inhabitants. As the characters struggle to define their individuality and reconcile their ideals with ordinary life, we are witness to their unique self-discoveries. At times mournful and haunting, this story collection celebrates the nobility of simple life, of striving and failing without ever losing hope.

Ooligan Press • Portland, Oregon • ooligan.pdx.edu

Available May 2013 from Ooligan Press

Up Nights

**a novel
by Daniel Kine**

fiction | $13.95 | 200 pages
5" × 8" | softcover | ISBN: 978-1-932010-63-3

OOLIGAN
PRESS

Up Nights Daniel Kine's second book, is a classic road novel for a new generation. In raw, unrelenting prose, Kine tells the story of the complexities of human relationships when four friends embark on an existential journey through the underbelly of society. As they drift from city to city, they each struggle to connect with the disenchanted people they encounter along the way. *Up Nights* speaks to the reality of the human condition: the unequivocal impermanence of life.

Ooligan Press • Portland, Oregon • ooligan.pdx.edu

American Scream: Palindrome Apocalypse

by Dubravka Oraić Tolić

poetry | $14.95
240 pages | 6" × 9" | softcover
ISBN: 978-1-93-201010-7

Utopia—we all want our own, but who pays for it and at what price? Croatian poet Dubravka Oraić Tolić delivers a masterful, thought-provoking answer with exquisite language and imagery in the epic poem *American Scream*. Complementing *American Scream* is *Palindrome Apocalypse*—a palindrome that is artful in both technique and story—presented side-by-side with the Croatian original to preserve its visual effect. Together, Oraić Tolić's poems explore dark themes of social and individual selfishness in pursuit of dreams and the unintended consequences of those efforts; examine the tension between a nation's dream of freedom and the outworking of that dream; capture the heart of pre- and post-war Croatia, yet speak universally of the pain of bringing one's visions to life.

Dot-to-Dot, Oregon

by Sid Miller

poetry | $13.95
88 pages | 6" × 9" | softcover
ISBN: 978-1-93-201029-9

Sid Miller explores seven routes from the coast to the mountains, from inner-city Portland to the Idaho border. *Dot-to-Dot, Oregon*, a collection of fifty poems, travels through the cities, towns, and monuments of Oregon. Using these locales as a background, three voices narrate the author's loving but critical relationship with the state he calls home.

"Connect the dots? If you do you'll discover some strange and wonderful constellations superimposed over familiar topography... *Dot-to-Dot* is a lyrical and, at times, a dark and hilarious guide to the blue lines (secondary roads) of the Beaver State. So before you head out to Shoetree (Don't look for it on a highway map.), Nyssa (a damsel in metaphysical distress?), or some other exotic location in the Beaver State, take a look at Sid Miller's new book or, better yet, take it with you on your rambles."

— Carlos Reyes

Ooligan Press • Portland, Oregon • ooligan.pdx.edu

Killing George Washington:
The American West in Five Voices
by Anne Jennings Paris

poetry | $13.95
120 pages | 6" × 9" | softcover
ISBN: 978-1-93-201030-5

Killing George Washington tells the story of the American frontier as it moves west. Anne Jennings Paris, in a collection of narrative poems, imagines the voices of the forgotten historical figures of Lewis Wetzel, a notorious Indian killer; York, the slave who accompanied Lewis and Clark; Charity Lamb, Oregon's first convicted murderess; Ing Hay, a Chinese immigrant who made a name for himself as a doctor; and Mary Colter, an architect who helped shaped the western landscape. Exploring the American consciousness, these poems question our shared heritage through the personal stories of legends.

Oregon Stories
Edited by Ooligan Press

poetry | $16.95
272 pages | 6" × 9" | softcover
ISBN: 978-1-932010-33-6

This collection of 150 personal narratives from everyday Oregonians explores the thoughts, feelings, and experiences of the people who live in this unique state. *Oregon Stories* shows why people cherish this state and why Oregonians strive to keep Oregon unique and beautiful while celebrating its rich history and diverse opportunities. Drawn from the Oregon 150 Commission's Oregon Stories website project—in which a variety of citizens submitted personal stories that will resonate with any Oregon resident—this book collects the stories and histories of the people that make this place home. The subject of these stories varies widely—some authors tell detailed family histories, while others describe exciting travels throughout Oregon's beautiful landscape. This book features local contributors who reside in different communities all over the state, resulting in a publication truly representative of Oregonians as a whole. Read much more about the Oregon Stories project as part of the Oregon 150 Official Sesquicentennial Commemoration on the main website.

Ooligan Press • Portland, Oregon • ooligan.pdx.edu

You Have Time for This:

Contemporary American Short-Short Stories

Edited by Mark Budman & Tom Hazuka

fiction | $11.95
135 pages | 5" × 7½" | softcover
ISBN: 978-1932010176

Love, death, fantasy, and foreign lands, told with brevity and style by the best writers in the short-short fiction genre. *You Have Time for This* satiates your craving for fine literature without making a dent in your schedule. This collection takes the modern reader on fifty-three literary rides, each one only five hundred words or less. Mark Budman and Tom Hazuka, two of the top names in the genre, have compiled an anthology of mini-worlds are as diverse as the authors who created them. Contributing writers include Steve Almond, author of *My Life in Heavy Metal* and *Candyfreak*; Aimee Bender, author of *The Girl in the Flammable Skirt*; Robert Boswell, author of five novels, including *Century's Son*; Alex Irvine, author of *A Scattering of Jades*; L. E. Leone, who writes a weekly humorous column about food and life for the *San Francisco Bay Guardian*; Justine Musk, author of dark-fantasy novels, including *Blood Angel*; Susan O'Neill, writer of nonfiction and fiction with a book of short stories called *Don't Mean Nothing; Short Stories of Vietnam*; and Katharine Weber, author of several novels, including *Triangle*. From Buddha to beer, sex to headless angels, there's a story here for everyone. In *You Have Time for This* you will find: flash fiction from forty-four authors, works from across the globe, highly regarded authors from all types of genres, fresh work from emerging writers, and fifty-three stand alone pieces that tie the world together.

Enjoy. You have time for this.

"A really good flash fiction is like a story overheard at a bar—personal, funny, dangerous, and sometimes hard to believe. *You Have Time for This* distills those qualities and many others into quick tall tales by writers who are as talented as they are magical."

—Kevin Sampsell, author of *Beautiful Blemish* and publisher of Future Tense Publishing

Ooligan Press • Portland, Oregon • ooligan.pdx.edu

Write to Publish

annual publishing conference hosted by

OOLIGAN
P R E S S

http://ooligan.pdx.edu/w2p/

Write to Publish is unlike any writing conference you've previously attended. Instead of focusing on the craft of writing, we explore the process of getting published.

The panels will host a variety of authors who will speak about their own experiences in publishing. These topic-led discussions are intended as an "industry mingle" with a Q & A. The authors will focus on the ups and downs, challenges, and triumphs they experienced in their careers. Local vendors from the publishing industry will also be present, sharing their knowledge and services with conference-goers.

Write to Publish is about empowering you as a writer so that you are one step closer to getting published. Get ready to spend a day having your questions answered and seeing how you, too, can become a published author.

Ooligan Press • Portland, Oregon • ooligan.pdx.edu

CPSIA information can be obtained at www.ICGtesting.com
Printed in the USA
BVOW010440190313

315852BV00003B/10/P